killarnoe

BOOKS BY SONNET L'ABBÉ

A Strange Relief (2001)
Killarnoe (2007)

killarnoe

POEMS

SONNET L'ABBÉ

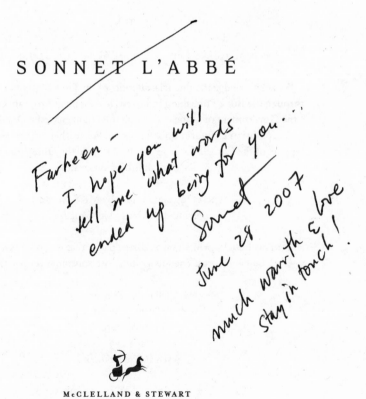

Farheen –
I hope you will
tell me what words
ended up being for you...
Sonnet
June 28 2007
much warmth & love
stay in touch!

McCLELLAND & STEWART

Library and Archives Canada Cataloguing in Publication

L'Abbé, Sonnet
Killarnoe : poems / by Sonnet L'Abbé.

ISBN 978-0-7710-0677-7

I. Title.

PS8573.A156K54 2007   c811'.6   C2007-900050-9

We acknowledge the financial support of the Government of Canada
through the Book Publishing Industry Development Program and that of
the Government of Ontario through the Ontario Media Development
Corporation's Ontario Book Initiative. We further acknowledge the
support of the Canada Council for the Arts and the Ontario Arts Council
for our publishing program.

Typeset in Haarlemmer by M&S, Toronto
Printed and bound in Canada

This book is printed on acid-free paper that is 100% recycled,
ancient-forest friendly (100% post-consumer recycled).

McClelland & Stewart Ltd.
75 Sherbourne Street
Toronto, Ontario
M5A 2P9
www.mcclelland.com

1 2 3 4 5   11 10 09 08 07

to my like
to my unlike

this dissociative fugue

Because it is out there (orchid) outside your and, *it is.*

– Anne Carson

When they torture you | too bad | to talk | plant a tree.

– Alice Walker

Tra-la-la-la-la.

– Alice Walker

Contents

AHEM:AMEN

OLD SOUL

I was born looking for.
Somehow I came here.

I followed the promise
of collisions, cubisms,

to a pronged, arboreal truth
not strung out from spools

of old syntax. An insight
outside the senses. A tasted

image. A colour heard.
Not for comfort.

Okay, for a kind of comfort.
For a synesthesia. Something

amniotic. A memory before form,
the infinite inside the integral.

How else can I put it?
For the spirit prism, written.

REPETITION

The sound of the drum
means the teller's gonna come.
    The teller's gonna come.
    The teller's gonna come.

The sound of the drum
means the teller's gonna come.
    The teller's gonna come.
    The teller's gonna come.

Hear the hollow sound
from a skin above a round
and a hand slapping circles
at the sky

Feel the way your feet
on the ground will mark the beat
and how the tapping trip
can get you high

You hear my peace propaganda?
    this is my peace propaganda
Come hear my peace propaganda
    this is my peace propaganda

Close your eyes and feel
how the rhythm helps to heal
the cacophony of crap
inside your head

And be aware of he
who says repeat after me

Follow only if you won't be
blindly led

This is my peace propaganda
I don't know but I been told
Come hear my peace propaganda
people buy what they are sold

PRONOUNCEMENT

What was is over.
What is is busy being.

What will be is willed
to us by the endlessly revising
pen of circumstance;
our own will a fiction
that can still move.

I may be
because of Catullus,
but what propelled
each syllabus
through his fruitful quill?

Sometimes I wish
I could witness
the simultaneous births
of languages,
to be in all
those places at that once.

Was one grunt
spun out into countless tongues?

Or did all argot grow
from separate sprouts
in the coincident ground
of our many mouths,
momentous as a season's dandelions
wordsporing the wind?
Did Earth's whole surface
wake, shaken,

from deep linguistic winter
into speech's spring?

My tongue
but one
leaf of this arbus, conscious, rustling
in the unhistoric event
of our happening.

HUMAN

Okay, spirit. Quiet.
Will you recognize yourself?

Be intimate and intelligent,
with me.
Now, now.

Realize this,
in this quietful process,
this meaningful place
I release to,
(as I strive in all directions)
I am kind, not harmless.

None of us
comes here unarmed.

Let's drop our swords.
Let's drop our my pen is
mightier than yours.

Now.
Together. Team?

Let's identify the children.
Let's show the blank and open ones

what one's sound,
one's say-so,
can mean.

INSTRUMENTAL

MA

Ma, ma, ma.
Raw formed emanation.
Mama mimesis?
Yes, mom imitation.

You am, gummy mammal.
Mammary yum?
Aureolar ohm.
Mmm hmm, little one.

WAAANH

Goddess – I want – to kill you
so you won't – move –
But I weigh six pounds
and for now hold on – to you
for my goddamn – life –

Help me, abandoner –
I can't – control you –
If only I could – rise from this
powder-scented pen

I'd sharpen these tiny – nails
to claws, unsheath – my teeth
from these soft – gums, leap
upon you – tear you open

and suck – you dry – you abhorrent
package – of pure love –
force your attention
on the – purity – of my desire –

curse – how you *unthinkingly* withhold
what I want – with every atom
of my freshfallenness –
with your casual, easy – look –

                                    away

AH

An open moment,
a prolonging
of notice
without reaction, a downward
fountain of data, filling.

Unclosing, throat's
wholeness, wide,
to swallow
the thrall of all of it:
full bulge of gulp
held —

nothing undulating, no
void vacuum
pursuing a present cud
through
a human tunnel.

Sustained hum,
sustenance
pouring, not pulsing.

Rinse without erosion,
flush without the closed
push of peristalsis.

Clarity
not needing blur
to know itself.

UH

The shyness, the delay to say
I'm thinking, I'm processing,
the silence before the words
string into coherence that I can't leave
unfilled, all my ignorance,
the mice scurrying in the maze,
please wait while the images
load, sound saying I'm not
                         dumb

or the coyness, the delay to say
I'm answering, when I'm processing
the first thought into a string of words
less hurtful, less assessing,
less revealing of the blunt fact
of my unkindness, all my interiority,
the scurry to hide it behind my back
please wait while I remember
your heart, sound the safety on a sharp
                         tongue

OOH

noteworthy
the pure ooh
of boo
of moo

the poor ooh
of few
of zoo

scary
the through ooh
of room
of pool

the rued ooh
of oops
of fool

(un)impressive
the ew ooh
of goo
of poo

the woo ooh
of swoon
of cool

awful
the flute ooh
of moon
of true

the mute not-two
of who
are you

OH

((((o)))))

this o is my throat
this o is my oh yeah
this o is my really
this o is my credulousness

((((o))))

this o is my soundful closed
this o is my politeness
this o is my mask
this o is my feigned interest

(((o)))

this o is my I see
this o is the shared place
this o is my sympathy
this o is my mistake

((o))

this o is my aha
this o is my incredulousness
this o is my startling backward
this o is our otherness

(o)

this o is just o
this o is symbolic sound
this o is the presence of nothing
this o is common ground

o

this o is my lips
this o is my gentle kiss
this o is my suckling
o my greedy tenderness

oh
uh-oh
oh

I

doesn't sound like it looks.

A is ah, but Ih isn't I.
A is ay, but Iy isn't I.

Aye is I.
And eye is I.
In a way,
even Y is I.

Effortwise,
a sigh is I.
Emotionally,
to cry is I.
And existentially
to why is I.

To another, *Ich* is I.
Je is I, or *Cho* is I.
Na is I, or *Yo* is I.

We chose a diphthong.
Don't know why.

DUH

1. (n) an idiot, numbskull, etc.
e.g., You're such a ~.
2. (expl) That statement is obvious.
e.g., A. Apples are fruits. B. ~!
or I was like, ~ !

See also, hello-o!?!?

No shit.
Keep up.

The trick of it
is on the tongue tip.
Cup of glottal stop.
Oral lock and pop.

Spilled or skipped
off the lip,
rhythmic non sequitur
is quick-witted quip.

Sophisticated la-dee-dah.
Boardroom, backroom
nyah, nyah, nyah.

Riff on this
lingual fricative lick.
Sink or swim
in conversational clique.

Suck it up, spirit.
Hello-o. Get hip.

[here is a picture of the me I cannot hide]

If you think I will dignify that
with a response,

you're right. That resonates.
I thought I'd thought that thought,

but you thought it through
more simultaneous dimensions.

Are we just chemical reactions,
mattering? Happy, then unhappy

consequences of nuclear fission?
Yes, but – But what?

What is gravity grasping for?
Why does it cling to us so gently?

If only all decisions were as polar
as yes/no. Our oscillations

between clustered possibilities
diffuse our intent. Think about it.

But don't think about it too much.
Never give up? Learn to let go?

At what level of cellular being
do we doubt? Who knows.

Right now I just need to sit and be
vertebrate, forgive myself

my limited range of perception,
disorganize myself into the simplicity

of atoms. Feel all points of contact,
and let question be drained out,

drawn out of our surface existence
on this little blue particle,

drawn through the crystal logic of rock
down into the burning brilliance

of our core. Let the mind move toward
that centre, that immeasurable origin

that is there, by infinite degrees – there –
more accurately, more minutely

and more consciously
than my best conceived and argued

point.

UNGH

please no
yes no

do it no that way
whiplash yeah whip like
teeth tear
flesh from bone

come on
come *on*

now before I submit
to the thug weight
the rival little bitch
of your will

get over here
and make me grunt
do what I tell you
make me suck

bring it, favourite
I'm begging you, toy
bring your fucking tenderness
here right now

no oh I suffer
no it's too good
oh it's too bloody
it's too cunt! bloody! good!

SHH

shush, sugar, hush
this heartthrash,
this sharp anxious mess
shall pass

o shyness, the blush
at shit and needing to wash it,
at shit and wanting to share it,
of wishing

our piss flushed
and shame quashed,
the rush of passions surety
brushes off and brashness

shuns, the gush
of harshness
through the mesh of fiction
between he and she;
let me cushion it,

let me freshen,
let me witness your shit
and keep you, unshunned

let me be shore
to your ashes,
let me show mushy, luscious
shamelessness
in the crush of my lips
to your ferocious
                    flesh

ow

No, by now
I know
your blows
wanted sound.

Now I won't
moan or shout.
I give up
no more ground.

I don't disclose
or avow
what fouls at
five years old

I had to
allow.
On I go. Older.
Controlled. Proud.

And if these sound
poems
expose a noise
I still can't keep down,

so?
You don't follow
poems. And you won't
ever own how

my sorrow
learned to love itself
in the hollow
of vowels.

La, la, la.
Don't listen, hon.
Lullaby lulls.

La, la, la
little one.
Lullaby unswerves.

La, la, la
baby.
Lullaby cusps.

La, la, la,
my love.
Lullaby realiiiiiiiiiiiiiiiiiiiiiiiigns.

TEN VARIATIONS ON HA

FRIENDS

If they say that to you
then they are not your friends.

What should I have called them, then?
Classmates?
Acquaintances?
In kindergarten?

I knew their names.
We were together
six hours each day.

Who else but friends
got close enough
to whisper all your uglinesses
in your ear?
Then asked
to borrow your special pen?

I needed other names
for them.

BODY SHOP

Your body's got the wrong features?
Oh, wainh, wainh!

Its finish isn't status tint?
You wanted
the other coupling link?

I don't see a problem.
Gets you from A to B.
Has all the usual sensory
inputs and outputs.
And size is no indicator
of performance.

So it's not meant
for the fast lane.
Soon you'll get used to
how it drives, and forget
you ever wanted
the bells and whistle.

And if you think your ride
has anything to do
with how easily you score,
well –

Who ordered it, then?
Doesn't matter.
You can't return it here.

ZEBRAS

do zebras
have solid parents
a black stallion
a white mare

are they black
horses with
white stripes

or white
horses with
black bars

if you see them
in cages
at just the right
angle

will they seem
a uniform colour
lose their
prison suits

does chocolate milk
come from
brown cows

my sister and I
were young
and thought
along those lines

MY SONNETINA

My pretty mind.
My pretty mind.
See how pretty it is?
Tell me again.

Is it not a white lotus?
opening –
an infinite crinoline,
(un)veiling –

Tell me again.

Inspires the aroma
of harmonious tones.
Disassembles red.
Disassembles blue.

Takes oral delight.
Opens aural unboundary.
Quickens clitoral intellectuality.
Makes mathematic sense:

This beautiful void.

Knowing its own thought
like echoes
as this polarized cellular collective
senselessly grasps
at its perceptions.

(You don't know.)
(You'll never know.)

My pretty mind.
My pretty mind.
See how pretty it is?
I know: it's as pretty
as a sunkiller

inside the prisonword
of rose.

THEORY, MY NATURAL BROWN ASS

I've paid for too many degrees,
posited too many historical positions,
made too many semiotic apologetics,
forwarded far too many feminist responses
to too many textual materialities

to have an ass this big.

In theory, my ass
does not signify.

But this insistence of the body,
this non-linguistic expression
of inertia and caloric lust,
is a corporeal truth that mental exercise
can't deconstruct.

Or is it just an inverted absence?
The presence of the lack
of any Aryan heritage?

I'm the post-colonial girl
who went abroad and squatted and lunged
while the maid, snapping out
wet laundry, watched.
Skinny brown bitch, was what I thought!
The poor men looked at my ass
like it was a pair of Boston Cremes.

But I was raised
on white girls' dreams.
This juicy back might fly in hip hop,
but I meant to fit

into tinier social circles,
and JLo's butt's already taking up
two stools at the representation bar.
Missy E's already gone
bonh bo bonh bonh
all the way to the bank.

My ass doesn't give a shit
that my mind is post–Third Wave.
It is imperialist, a booty-Gap,
expanding into a third space: the place
beyond my seams. Who cares
that sizes are all "seems" anyway:
you shop, you walk
the slippery significatory slope
on which an S, M, or L might fall.
The mall

is the spatial organization
of desire, I know, but
does that make my ass look small?

MY MS. POST-UNIVERSE

I want world peace.
Tee-hee!

Um, if the planet is our
collective home,
then isn't all labour, all trade,
domestic?

Maybe it's just me.

Why aren't trees the governance board
that sets our global agenda?
Solid returns of their varying green
our mission statement?
See how seasonally they agree?

Tee hee!

Isn't money codified love?
Codified focused energy?

Aren't 2-D, linear models
an ego distortion of a dimensionless
real? And my double Ds
the perfect biotech model
of care delivery?

Uh, the grasping pedophilic moment,
I think, is a precise
limit of rational argument.
I'm pretty sure it's the violent waking
of the collective unconscious.
And polite aversion's censorious urge

no match for our sucking, baby,
doll-addiction. Whee!

I wish I could implant
the megatits
to distract from the global power play.
Be the tight wideopen pinnacle
for which the winners climb and pay.
Sit atop the glory ladder,
lay back under their motherhunger
and take it, take it,

for a fee.

I'd pull an endless train to retrain
child armies
in defensive strategy.
Fund the protection of their open hearts.
Do porn for charity.

Oh, Great Daddy!
Why else did You give me
this divine mindbody?
I just want to make You happy.

So let's play world peace!
Wanna theorize rape fantasy with me?

Tee hee!

MY PERFEKT SOLDJA

iz a kwik wit.
She sharpen her tung
an call it.

Not-knowin: schoopidity.
Kryin: whinin.
Want: weakness.
Protess: tsch, a likkle vex.

Dose tear in da sandbox
were grit in she eye.
Girl chile prodigy
in dafensive manoeuva.

She love a sore spot
made to grovel. Loneliness
she bloodlet, den string
it empty skull aroun she neck.
You dare leak da secret
o she self-contanement?
She laugh and laugh
at she own in-joke.

She got a hairtrigga yes,
unsaftied. She long ago XXX
off da no zones,
an put up barb-wire fence
along da border o kweschun.

Sewn up tight, not uptight.
Girl can alwayz let loose on brew,
and mess it up mess it up!
for da rightchuss, winnin team.

It da angers lockt
in every blud red cell
dat burn. Terroristz
o she hi-price peace.
Dey pretenn to sleep.
But at nite
dey karve dey sullen inshials
inta she soft inside.

Dey wimper inside, and annoy.
She try to bind and gag dem.
She hate how
dey jump up, mad barking
at any sudden movement.

She goin beat
and drug dem again, soon.

Wen dey finally die
she gwine be klean and ready!
To storm da field
o soshial funkshun! To klimb
da obstakuls to powa!

To target an elimanate
da foolish perpetratorz
o she dezire.

A fierce calmness. Heat rises a bubble to the surface,
two. Baby orbs hover on the sweet pool's face

then pop. Pop. Lightness comes together to sound
its disperse. Makes way for the next round

of roundnesses amid the liquid. Red, somewhere.
Fuel to the fire. Pain without a nerve to tear

through. Shimmer at the film simmers from its depth,
the roil and rumble turning over, space tests its breadth

in kick thrash gasps. A fist in the soft wall.
A heel in the flesh. Contracts and expanses. Swells

that crest and break in a wash of horsepower,
anger like a motor carrying, a motor hauling, shower

of meteors splashing hot crowns of plasma
way up there, somewhere a layer of my atmo

sphere is absorbing a rain of shrapnel, cushioning
shards like broken glass pushed into an ocean.

The flush of soft swirls ebb and eddy, fractals
of cause and effect. The knock of one molecule

on another sending single clicks curling, tendrils
of a hard slap on distant skin spiral and cool

then are picked up at the helictical core,
and hibernate in its genomic fold until once more

some jagged trauma shakes the cone of seed. We need
to burst our violence into sparks of light, or bleed.

Male bride, you are not ordered. Invited. A warm body is your ring.
Male wife, work and love me. Outside and inside a home.
Male nurse, care is not an industry. You olympic, amateur Father.
Male cunt, stop laughing at arousal's earnest posture.
Male bitch, state what you want. Learn the honest quiet of athleticism.
Male pussy, tears do signal the hit on a set heart.
Male diva, sad show of neck bling, that expensive string of girls.
Male chick, keep shaving, keep grooming, keep breeding.
Male slut, ew! Dirty cheques, dirty!
Male madam, redecorate your sweatshop. Think feng shui.
Male hag, poor bespectacled librarian of porn.
Male princess, who will rescue you from sick coach's corporate
    locker room?
Male sister, beauty is your slow smile. Eye lock. Ageless deep breath.
Male mother, I see bridges and roads. Electric light. Hot water.
Male daughter, innocence falls. Learns to get back up.
Male friend, don't we shoulder our masculinities together?
Male female, behold:

MY MME GANDHI

j'suis mme Gandhi
j'suis revenue ici
tu te rapelles?
tu te repelles de moi?

j'suis revenue ici
vous parler aujourd'hui
comme frère
avec fraternité

nous sommes vos soeurs
monsieurs
nous sommes vos coeurs
monsieurs

vous nous avez eu
nos corps vous ont pas plus
des jouets avec joues
maintenant vous ne jouez plus

(comment m'as-tu laissée
comme ça?
comment ça se fait
que tu m'as laissée comme ça?)

si vous (voulez)
aidez nous, mesdames
si nous (voulons)
aidons-vous, messieurs

je suis venue ici
pour vous dire aujourd'hui
je suis
mme Gandhi

z: GHAZALS FOR ZAHRA KAZEMI

One definition of the word ghazal *[is that it] is the cry of the gazelle when it is cornered in a hunt and knows it will die.*

– Agha Shahid Ali

The poem has no palpable intention upon us. It breaks, has to be listened to as a song: its order is clandestine.

– John Thompson

Alpha male, Zahra.
Zeta female, Zahra?

Nine eleven I noticed mom's name is Zalena.
I noticed my cuzzins, Zaibun and Farzeen.

A to Z, said my uncle Asad.
Yes, Adam, said Muhammad.

The mountain comes. Zero sum.
Abu Ghraib. Arar.

Gaza, Zahra. Bloody gauze.
Your gaze on a military strip.

Ra, ra. Sis boom bah.
Hip: hype: hip. Hooray!

This fall season, let's pump
iron. Push artillery chic

(bodycheck them) on petite puck chicks.
Bench the liberal press.

Pompom the pill-fed population.
Pep the house-poor on.

The strong's odds, yawn.
Big bad opponent, rad rally.

CBC says A B C.
Hanguk says ka na da.

Yo, yo. That last book said Aral.
Look, Karakalpak, it said!

Nunavut says Kashechewan.
Toronto says uh-uh, ka-ching.

Ottawa spells inukshuk.
Quebec tells them phoque.

In any cab, hear a-salaam alaykum.
North Amerika, say alaykum a-salaam.

I say, old chap, you're jolly mum.
Muss use ainshen Chinee watoh torchoh.

Say ah. Say yassa, massa. Say uncle.
Learn 21 moans that drive men crazy!

Zat is ze wrong answer. Ve haff vays
of making you talk.

Ten Hail Marys, child. Two Our Fathers.
La la la la la la, I can't hear you . . .

Yo G. Dis bitch front wen she wan freak. Word.
Swear, your honour. Lynndie never said
                              mwa-ha-ha, mwa-ha-ha.

How I use you, too, Zahra.
Me, a name I call my self. Fatwa, a note.

Capitalizing on the buzz of your was.
A Jezebel with my new Uzbek

while oil's gazillions upholster plush pews.
Ohm, Zahra. Reason, Zahra. Shalom, inshallah, amen.

My life of ease. How can I please
when your pleas track my waking dreams?

Mirror. Image. Other, Zahra. My body
can't stop recognizing – realizing – itself.

MY INNER CITY

OPEN LETTER

I want to offer my apologies
to you, whoever you are.

You don't know me.
Right now you're flailing to get free
of a cage named belief
or pain or immediate need,
probably aiming your justified rage
at someone closer,
someone visible, or
if there are
no moving targets within your range

then inward, where
your anger
can fling its tiny arrows
all along the bloody corridors
of intestines, nerves, and veins.

I want to say I'm sorry
for all the ways I keep you there.
For all the days I reach
for more than my share.
Everyone here has more than theirs,
so that a smaller more seems poor.
We don't compare our shares
to yours.

I can't undo what's been done
by those who came before.
Please know I stone myself
with hard words
like "cog" or "whore."

If I had the key, I'd send it.
"Make copies for your friends!"

Instead I hope it helps to say:
equilibrium does keep score.
Have mercy on me.
I know
your cage isn't imagined.

Imagination is its door.

TONE

is an important aspect
of any class text. Ask
your professor if you may
say *no way!* to object, or
hey! to interject, in any essay
meant to earn respect.

You can't say: *this dude
knows his shit*. Nor can you
say: *he's full of it*. To argue
your point, your joint
gotta have vocab game.

However and *nonetheless*
kick *but*'s ass. They got
up-in-front-of-the-class.
Address to impress.
Your convention hall pass.

The rules of tone are all
unspoken. One learns
the hard way
how they can be broken.

POOR SPEAKER

I understand you.
I get what you're trying to say.
What you're trying to say is you want me to get it.

I get it. You want me
to understand. You want me to know
not the words, but what's behind them. Got it.

You're trying to tell me
what you want me to hear. What I
hear is all words, but that's not all there is.

I totally comprehend.
There's a comprehensive totality
beyond, or above, or within, or outside

whatever you just said.
Yes, yes. Your vocabulary can't put the nuance
on the fine feeling you wish to express.

Not that you're feeling fine, I know.
Rather, the feeling is fine like a fine point. Right.
That's the point. I get it. If you could say so, you would.

You still want me to understand?
I told you from the beginning. I'm with you.
I got it. Why keep going on? It's gotten. It's all good.

MY OSAMA BIN LADEN T-SHIRT

It sits in the drawer.
What is it for?
What is it for?

See how blue his eyes are?
The benevolent, Christ-like smile?
Above his head, his turban
curves a clean white halo glow.

On the back, a night-vision
through rifle's sights:
the pair of towers caught within
a pale green circle on black –
America Under Attack!

I bought it in Korea.
A man under an overpass
was selling U.S. army surplus
out of the back of a truck.

It came home at the bottom
of my suitcase. No wands
nor X-rays picked it up.

ii

The tag says:
Care on Reverse.

X over the iron,
X over the bleach.
Universal symbols.

Despite the warnings,
I machine-washed it.
Tumbled it dry.

It survived.

iii

One Halloween,
Jerry wore it under a green flak jacket
with an embroidered Uzbek cap.
I dressed in my own brown skin, in silk hijab
and a kaftan I got at Goodwill.

Young boys eyed us on the streetcar.
I had Jerry button his coat.
Suddenly naked in public
with that scarf around my head.

At the party, people I'd never met
didn't know I was dressed up.
Are you John Walker Lindh?
they asked Jerry.

We stood together and waved
the little American flags
we bought in Chinatown.

We're Americans, we said.

It's the same old joke.
No costume equals serial killer, right?
Get it? We look just like everyone else?

iv

My Osama bin Laden
T-shirt
sits in the drawer.
What is it for?
Will it ever get worn out?

I don't think that kind
brown face can see
the light of day.

So sometimes I sleep in it.
Sometimes I pray.

FREESTYLE (ON WHY THEY DON'T LIKE HIP HOP)

The rhythm scares them.
It's too much like propaganda,
not enough like a march,
its public enmity too focused
and far too audible.

Our boys sure can't dance,
nyuk, nyuk!
like house letters,
like a fucking badge.

Those strange slurs, ebonic
consonants disappearing,
ghost words, code
among those who openly own
their unsold flesh.
Old souls on speaking terms.

They'll call it anything but ours.
They'll call it anything but art.

The Jacksons go supernova
interpellating us all
into the rhythm nation. Then
another expensive education wins
a T.S. Eliot prize for saying anew,
not me.

"You speak so well!"
Chris Rock wants to crack
skulls. He won't stop

saying motherfucker. Pryor's
propped up somewhere,
drooling some garbled hope,
still crass as hell.

STUPID LOVE SONG

I'm in love with a stupid man
How stupid, how stupid is he?
He can't say "supposedly"
he can't sing a note
he can't stop loving me.

I'm in love with a stupid man
How stupid, how stupid am I?
I must be stupid
If I think he's stupid
yet can't find a better guy.

I'm in love with a stupid man
How stupid, how stupid is he?
I tell him he's stupid,
he tells me he's not
then pours me a cup of tea.

I'm in love with a stupid man
How stupid, how stupid am I?
I always wanted
the quick-tongued kind
but they always made me cry.

I'm in love with a stupid man
How stupid, how stupid is he?
Goes to work every day,
falls hard into bed,
says his prize is my company.

I'm in love with a stupid man.
How stupid can you get?
I've tried to dump him

A million times
But he hasn't left me yet.

How could I love a stupid man?
How stupid could I be?
I might be stupid
but only he's stupid
enough to keep loving me.

Well, I'm trying my best
to stay off the dope,
but reality

is a stiff hit
to take
without a mixer.

How fog softens
sharp focus!
Blessedly blunts

incisive sight!
The fuck of it is
I mean to give

clear witness.
And the sobering
truth

is that the daybuilding,
self-conscious,
American goal

sees me as variant,
deviant,
a representational

lie. My dark part
will not yet stand
for our idolized

whole. A part
of us wishes
I'd die. So instead

of banging
my head
against towering

ideal-walls, instead
of suicidally crashing
that blissful Other-

ignorance party,
I'll fly
an alternate plane

into my own madness.
I'll kill off,
muzzle, euthanize

my ethical heart,
ghettoized.
I confess

I'm compelled
to cross via cannabis
the conceptual lines

between fiction
and fact,
us and them,

stoned and sober,
rational and
criminal mind.

Isn't high even,
isn't high level
with an overseeing,

elite, oblivious,
law-writing,
hardwired, happy,

discriminating,
dominant eye?
I too want to believe

everything
I hear me
telling myself,

I want what is
beautiful
to be just what (I say it)

is. Reckless?
Must poems
be my most

policed territory?
Ought I to edit here
nerves' weak

need to observe
a moment of weed-
uncensorship?

Protect my peace
agenda from the terror
of altered states?

Warning: I dream
the public page as
a (re)construction zone,

and language
the heavy machinery
I use to build

the inner world's
permanent
landmarks.

A freedom, a somewhere
I can be both
out there

and secure. So, Lord,
tell me the code
and I'll operate in it,

safely, squarely
and as faithfully
as the crane

that once soberly set
the steel, sure
beams

of the Trade Center.

BIPOLARITY

The long cubic
function of my mood.
Three axes:
space, moment, matter.

One arm reaches
along a gaseous blissness
the other approaches
the hardest nothingful hole.

The stupid numeracy
of the heartbeat's series,
the arbitrary meaning
of XX, XY.

Sleeping bodies
hard driven
by the Boolean beat
of ones and ohs, in me

the Fibonacci conscience
wakes weeping, shakes
the fractal, nervous
core geometry.

Water rises to the surface.
I apply the cold poultice
of rational logic, try to
freeze the ebb and flow,

but now yes, now no:
I think, therefore I think I know,
but am probably
just a Libran aggregate

dwelling on
the dangerous pore
of the origin.

A ROMANCE IN THREE ACTS

act one

Threes, he said.
Threes, I agreed.

The father, the son, the ghost.
The right, the left, the centre.
Before, during, and after.

Our meeting, our combining, our solution, he said.
You, me, and love.
Our meeting, our dancing, our separation, I said.
Situation, expectation, tragedy/comedy.

Threes, he seeded.
Threes, I watered.

act two

It's all in the threes, he sprouted.
Lucky 33 on his football jersey.
Three threes in his PIN.
Threes on the exactor,
box the trifecta,
threes on the Pro-Line long shot.

It is threes, I watered.
Black, white, grey.
Red, yellow, blue.
Mother, father, child.

(But in my head I was branching)
Funny how also black/white/indian.
Funny how also red, white, and blue.
Funny how also mother/father/other child.

Impulse, inhibition, (in)action.

act three

Event, witness, the historical account.
Pros, cons, the decision.

It's all threes, he leafed.

It's true,
but I'm sorry, I flowered
and fell. From here on in

I'm all about the nines.
I'm all about the Möbius strip
of nonic multiples.

Threes are true, but I leave them
for you.
I'll be about the nows
and the not-nows. I have to believe
(I have to believe)
in a looping, feminine heroic,
in zeros,

and the beautiful
(a)symmetry
of twenty-sevens.

WAVES

we are waves the mass radiation
we are waves the masculinear desire
we are waves in space an atom/ically
we are waves the plasmability of fire

we are waves amid the spill of liquid
we are waves through the chill crystal trees
we are waves on an ebonymy of absence
we are waves above the lightened normalties

we are waves the spring of the coil sprung
we are waves the wire's stubborn heart
we are waves the emblematic war's begun
we are waves the circularity of art

DETOX

I'm happy on apples.
A cherry jubilee.
Anus, esophagus, citrus-scrubbed.
I'm sparkling, grapefruit pink.

Is my bliss this unchemical?
Off the dirty thrill
of the sucrose roller coaster,
caffeine's race machinery unplugged,
I'm enough red meat for me.

There's nothing to wine about.
Last call for alcohol.
Weaned off nicotine, nope to dope –
it's a waking dream. Not-me.

Suddenly, I'm solid as a clean joke.
Stable as a wooden table.

The trees laugh like teenagers
at my clearly altered state.

REALIZATION

Welcome to happiness
that undiscovered –

it brings the other word
out and into the light.

Here, in the happiness
colours fall from the ordinary

out and up and wring
through the heart

like a companion, like a million
fairies of intelligence.

Light, the dark, like
the dark holding its cups

of shadow around the invisible,
the pairs of truths

with their facets sparkling.
Truths like smooth stones

sparking embers of consciousness
at the contact points.

It's here, in the awe of it,
as lonely of you as pain

so I thought it was pain.
Joy, doubling me over,

joy reaching through me
for a body to prop itself up.

AMNIOTIC

I'll
begin here.
Inside a vesica.
Transparent convex
spheroid suspended in
thixotropic white light. Viscous
love. All orifices awake. To sit on
the open mouth that kisses blood back
into earth. Head a tired tree made to fruit in all
seasons. Body wondering where abundance went.
Our dirty carbon metropoli. Glutineous, polymeric,
polluted. Anger and fear braving congestion. Red
corpuscles lined up grunting at the guttrough.
Synapses fire neon phosphorous guilt lights
overhead. Blink. Blink. Blink. Carnivorous
carnavalesque. Grr and the slit that
culminates. Whole world at
the chromosome tunnel.
Half of us open
directly onto
this.

THE THIRD BREAST

I noticed it first
after a night
in the wooded silence
that cuts across a still lake
cusped by pines.
I felt it out in the holy open
where a loon
echoes her sorrows
and the insides
of seeds all listen.

It looked
like an insect bite:
raised, red anger
under the cupped
curve of milk flesh.
I thought the forest's
piqued, entomologic mind
had stolen
away with its drop
of blood. But
no itch, just tenderness.

Then something like
a head.
What in there flamed?
White rebellion?
A mess of healing?
I tried to expel,
to puncture
the offensive swell.
Between my thumbs it gave up
as much liquid as a stone:

hardly, bloodless,
stubbornskinned,
moonthrobbing worry.

I retreated
and it calmed
to a dark purple
scare. A lump
of frighten.
A mark of if.
Silent in the busy
day, moaning
under the night's
wondering touch.

Scared, I cared.
My mute child,
I interpreted
its cry: it's not
sick, it's not
hungry: it just needs
to feel a love
on the outside
of being named.

Later, in between
spaces of wakefulness,
the breast
revealed itself:

budded off my rib,
it bobbed from
my chest. Pendulous
yet upturned, like
a cup of fresh.
Sienna acorn tip, sensitive
as a kiss

              recoil! at the mutate female
         body! Oh horrible extra
ecstasy! Nausea, vertigo
       oh flee, but where to go
                  where the body
          won't go also? Exorcise it,
             collapse it, lop it off

with a knife of white light –

Oh, but my love
for myself
made me sick. Love
enveloped all
of my soft folds,
love made room
for the ugliness.
Self-love welcomed
and petted the breast
like a stunted child.

Still dumb, numbed
against the wandering,
homeless rage evicted
into all my streams
from the untumour,
I fell against his love.
It held me up.

His ageless grey pity,
his evergreen owl eyes.
His love stroked my three
motherheads
and asked gently
if a tree knows
which are its extra limbs.

It's so old. Filling time starts and I'm all kitsched out. I can't
bring the nerve to the point of singing. Do you wish you were in
the fall, killing, will of all time? Wish the bring brought all it said
it would. Keep saying I and there's a wrongness in it. Try to stop
but it's a bad habit. You, who are you? You that I don't know and
never know but think is me and assume all my first persons are
somehow helpful.

~

These robot arms. Mechanical spinal twings. The backbreaking
moment of the ah like ah like that, oh. Why? Keep asking too
long and tears spin out as though from the original spiral itself.
The wrongness of the question wasn't true at that age. Are you
with me? You don't have to be. You already are. This step is not
parallel to anything. This comes in the darkest hours when your
sleep passes through me into my fingers and onto the page. You
dreamt these words eons and eons of future ago.

~

Da da da. Please forgive. Please don't look for syntactical some-
things where there are none. Now I'm thinking and hoping and
communication is only what we invented because of the break
of, the breach of, form. I've known this. Named my insides god
and won the incredulous pity. Such ungraspable allowing. Truth
ings from a lesser place than this, less crowned.

~

Dark spiral sounds from the disc that moves the world. Its terri-
ble vibrations aren't ours. Electron's dark path at greed pace, its
disappearance from itself, yet to return prodigal to our heart.

The millisecond of ourselves is fallen into the hands of hands. Sweet mercury of its telling. The naming of beauties and liminalities went into the forest and waited there to be cut down. Now it surges through feces and swirls in cables where it is digested into digital refuse.

~

Bright. King's ransom. Pure as ink. Waiting in the open moment for this. Porousness. Release and breathing into little baby belly. Cunt licking the cloth like a mouth. Tasting its veil. Grasping at the night under the sheet. Light, its lips, the ring of delicious expulsion. Like tubes of light hating our own ends, hating our orifices, the doors between sacred and named into boxes. Ah, to have the fronds waving, stems pulsing out from the split like green shoots diving up out of earth, to dig out the vee that never turned me upside up like this to forever be begging light from the hard, cold, calculating head.

The office girls. Had their hands over.
Their mouths tittering, at.

A photo of a disfigured.
Child when. I would not laugh.

They. Began. To kill
me with whispers I.

Escaped down a back. Stairwell
the door. Opened onto a winter.

Graveyard: the trees'. Branches.
Were black. Brushstrokes against

a grey. Sky I met. A kind. Man
he set an ornate. Wrought.

Iron cage upon the stone. Shelf
of a tomb. The cage was.

Filled with red. Birds he lifted.
The little, door and the birds.

Burst. Out, into, the air red.
Scraps. Grey sky.

Ribbons of glory red.
Falling twirling wheeling red.

Red birds like red leaves.
They congregated in the thin.

Bare black arms. Of a tree. Look.
I said the tree. Is a maple in fall

fire he struggled. To find his camera
and snap off. A quick shot

the birds scattered don't.
Worry he said. He had me.

Lift the little cage door one.
By one the birds. Gently.

Returned brown, sparrows and
one black, crow tried.

To enter but I knew.
Them by the strange buzz

of their. Wings I watched.
And shooed, it was not as.

Difficult as. I'd expected to keep.
The house of red birds pure.

MARS

Red planet, fire star.
Below the shoulder of the moon,
smaller than you are.

Old light, still moves.
Red sheep of the family,
what does your water prove?

Orange-cheeked war boy.
Dust storms. Your shores,
where our horses' souls are.

My own dream
was awake in the bedroom.

The rest of Ontario slept.
The walls' gyproc particles
watched, anger and fear
in their displaced granite hearts.

The hunted animal
that had paced for years
in the refuge
of my motionless body
was looking for its out.

Whatever had chased it
into the husk
of my unconscious
was not there.
It felt its moment of bravery.

Escape swelled upward
through my ribs
and forced back my head.
Flight surged out my eyes,
nostrils and mouth.
Coagulated for a moment
into a halo of light.

A red wolf.
She sat outside me, glowing
bloodred thanks.
How long had I been
her place of unforgetting?

She moved on
into the million miles
between a head
and its resting place.

My waking body
cavernous, now, emptied
of a red wolf's sadness.

CHORUS

Animals, all of us
Reading signs
Where is the animal
we left behind?

> Anima, animal, animus
> All of us
> Anima, animal, animus
> Minus, plus

Anima, animal, animus
All of us
Anima, animal, animus
Minus, plus

WHSHHH

by this dim moon's light
I invite you to my mind
we are meeting in a darkness
we are setting out to find

the words to the mission
we're supposed to set in motion
to retune imagination
to the rhythm of the ocean

the sea deeply wishes
it could speak so we hear
the waves of its wisdom
and the shivers of its fear

of what will come of moving
at a fibre-optic pace
we forgot what we are
when we conquered time and space

[the electronic drum's]
[steady beat becomes a hum]
[its velocity can speed]
[beyond a human spectrum]

[and I know how it feels]
[to ride that hyperbolic curve]
[up toward the top to tap]
[the supersonic nerve, but]

our bodies are organic
made of moon and sky and earth
we are travellers into death
we're emergers out of birth

and the water inside you
is the water in the sea
is the water in our pipes
and the water inside me

and the water inside you
is the water in the sea
is the water in our consequence
and the water inside me

and so the sea dreams
that we will run no faster
that we will stop our endless racing
to become each other's master

stop and hear the mission
we're supposed to set in motion
to retune imagination
to the rhythm of the ocean

know ourselves to be the heirs
of water, land, and air
we are sons of the sun
and the daughters of the sea

know ourselves to be the heirs
of water, land, and air
we are sons of the sun
and the daughters of the sea

DUMB ANIMALS

You don't want to read
this sequence. It's about us, I say.

I've read part, he says.
It's sad. Have you got a title yet?

It's about how hard it is to talk.
Dumb animal, was what I'd thought.

He smiled and shook his head.
Dumb *animals*, you mean, he said.

KILLARNOE

Killarnoe is a place I invented right
now. I just built it from my head. I started
with a letter k and set down the letters
that spilled out. What does that say when k-i-l-l

first sprouts? Something repressed, or
an instinct, that when allowed a moment's
free reign, opens to its own mind
and speaks bluntly? But see how I persisted

past the first impulse to slash at the page's
clean white throat, and instead adorned it
with a pretty vowel, gently drawing out the ells
to sulk the k down into a rumbled,

grudging argument against the mind's knee-
jerk proposal, the oh opening to compromise,
and a silent e watching without judgment.
Killarnoe, I decide, is the land

of our ancient people.

"Z: Ghazals for Zahra Kazemi"
Zahra "Ziba" Kazemi-Ahmadabadi (1949–July 11, 2003) was an
Iranian (Persian)-born freelance photographer and Canadian
citizen residing in Montreal who died in the custody of Iranian
officials following her arrest. Although Iran's regime insists
that her death was accidental, a former military staff physician
who left Iran and sought asylum in Canada in 2004 stated that
he examined Kazemi's body and observed evidence of rape
and torture.

"Zah"
In September 2002, Maher Arar, a Canadian software engineer,
was detained by U.S. Immigration officials during a stopover in
New York en route from Tunis to Montreal. Despite carrying a
Canadian passport, he was deported to Syria in accordance
with a U.S. policy known as "extraordinary rendition." Arar was
held in solitary confinement in a Syrian prison where he was
regularly tortured for almost a year, until his eventual release
and return to Canada in October 2003.

"Ze"
Lynndie Rana England is a U.S. Army reservist who served in
the 372nd Military Police Company and one of several soldiers
convicted by the U.S. Army in connection with the Abu Ghraib
torture and prisoner abuse in the Baghdad prison during the
Occupation of Iraq.

"My Osama bin Laden T-shirt"
John Phillip Walker Lindh (a.k.a. "The American Taliban") is an
American citizen who was captured during the 2001 invasion of
Afghanistan while fighting there for the Taliban. His capture
made worldwide headlines, and the media dubbed him "Johnny
Jihad," "Johnny Taliban," "Johnny bin Walker," and even "Ratboy."

ACKNOWLEDGEMENTS

This book was written with the support of the Toronto Arts Council and the Ontario Arts Council.

Poems from this collection have appeared in *Red Silk: An Anthology of South Asian Canadian Women Poets, Open Field: 30 Contemporary Canadian Poets, Short Fuse: The Global Anthology of New Fusion Poetry, Green Perspectives, The Literary Review of Canada, The Walrus Magazine,* and *Representative Poetry Online.*

Thank you to Priscila Uppal, George Elliott Clarke, and Molly Peacock, who read early drafts of this book. Thanks to Sina Queyras, Rishma Dunlop, Denis De Klerck, Todd Swift, Ian Lancashire, and Barbara Carey for publishing or broadcasting earlier versions of some poems. To Erina Harris, Gale Zoë Garnett, Diana Fitzgerald Bryden, Sandra Alland, Karen Mulhallen, Margaret Christakos, and Lee Gowan for their roles in seeing these poems performed.

Thanks to the women of the Salon for literary sensuality. To my students. And to all my colleagues at U of T.

To JS.

To Phedra and Jordan, mes chers semblables. And to the parental unit.